THE
BUDDHIST
MANDALA
POCKET COLORING
BOOK

Lisa Tenzin-Dolma

26 INSPIRING DESIGNS PLUS 10 BASIC TEMPLATES
FOR COLORING AND MEDITATION

WATKINS
Sharing Wisdom Since
1893

THE HEART OF STILLNESS

BUDDHIST MANDALAS ARE RICH WITH SYMBOLISM THAT CAN EVOKE MANY
DIFFERENT ASPECTS OF BUDDHIST TEACHING. HOWEVER, THEY ALWAYS
HAVE AN EMPHASIS ON THE STILLNESS AND PEACE AT THE CORE OF TRUTH.
ALTHOUGH THE WORLD IS A PLACE OF SUFFERING, MANDALAS ARE A PORTAL
THROUGH WHICH WE CAN TRANSCEND THAT SUFFERING. THROUGH THE JOY
OF PATTERN AND THE POWER OF MIND WE CAN ATTAIN FULFILMENT.

Buddhism traces its roots back to between 600BC and 500BC, when the Indian prince Siddhartha Gautama achieved a supreme state of enlightenment, after which he became a spiritual teacher known as the Buddha, or the "Awakened One". Having renounced luxury, he embarked on an enlightening quest around India to gain insight into the nature of suffering. He immersed himself in meditation and lived by the Middle Way—avoiding, after an unsatisfactory period of asceticism, the two extremes of self-indulgence and self-denial. During a period of deep meditation under the Bodhi tree in Bodh Gaya, in northern India, Gautama finally came to understand the truth of existence (*dharma*), and found release from the endless cycle of rebirth by entering *nirvana*: a sublime state of being.

The Buddha dedicated his life to teaching the dharma to others, and after his death his teachings were perpetuated through the establishment of temples and monasteries that embraced it. Buddhism flourished across Asia, yet gradually different schools developed. Basic principles were held in common by all the schools, yet individual practices and beliefs varied. There are two primary traditions of Buddhism: Theravada and Mahayana. Unlike followers of Theravada, Mahayana Buddhists believe in celestial buddhas and *bodhisattvas*—beings who can guide humans to a spiritual awakening. Bodhisattvas are already enlightened, yet out of compassion to humanity remain on Earth to help others. On finally reaching nirvana they become celestial buddhas and attain even greater powers. A pantheon of these beings developed, many of which are depicted in various forms of Buddhist art. These include mandalas, especially those that illustrate palaces of the gods.

Mandalas are an ancient Eastern art form, originating from around the 9th century. Traditional mandalas, often created by Buddhist monks, can be deeply elaborate representations of nirvana. The word mandala (a Sanskrit term meaning "circle" or

"THE LIGHT OF WISDOM CANNOT GROW
IN SUCH A MIND. THE SOLUTION TO THIS
PROBLEM IS MEDITATION."

LAMA YESHE

(1935–1984)

"CONCENTRATION IS ONE-POINTED,
FREE OF BAD THOUGHTS, AND WISDOM
DECIDES WHAT TRUTH REALLY IS."

NAGARJUNA

(150–250 AD)

"A MIND WHICH DWELLS UPON NOTHING
IS THE BUDDHA-MIND ... A MIND FREE
FROM DELUSION AND REALITY ALIKE."

HUI HAI

(720–814 AD)

"I HAVE DISCOVERED THIS PATH TO
ENLIGHTENMENT ... THERE AROSE IN ME VISION,
KNOWLEDGE, PENETRATION AND LIGHT."

SAMYUTTA NIKAYA

(6TH–5TH CENTURY BC)

"enclosure") was first recorded in the ancient Hindu scripture *Rig Veda*, but it is with the Buddhist tradition, in particular Tibetan Buddhism, that mandalas are most commonly associated. Mandalas derive from Eastern spiritual traditions and are considered maps of the cosmos. In meditation they act as a guide toward deeper self-understanding and ultimate truth. The cosmic diagram represents a sacred or spiritual realm through a pattern of symbolic, geometrically organized shapes and images—even celestial beings in certain Buddhist incarnations. In their imagery, mandalas reflect the macrocosm (the cosmos) and the microcosm (the mind and body of the individual). They provide an important aid to meditation, and a means of unifying macrocosm and microcosm; they awaken a person's spiritual energy and illuminate the path toward enlightenment.

The mandalas specially devised for this book, reflecting different aspects of Buddhist belief and tradition, are intended as simple tools for meditation—a key discipline of the dharma, embraced by all forms of Buddhism. Some of the mandalas are inspired by Tibetan originals, while others incorporate historic Buddhist symbolism, or employ a universal symbolism to which our conscious and unconscious minds will readily respond.

When selecting a mandala in this book to color in and use for meditation, just opt for one that appeals really strongly to you. All the mandalas are presented as line drawings. The first 26 designs, which are complex and sophisticated, are followed by a selection of basic geometrical templates you can elaborate to create your own design. Once you have chosen your mandala, let the recommended color palette guide you in deciding how to color it in; or alternatively, choose your own colors, following your intuition. When your mandala is colored to your personal preference, you can begin your meditation.

Meditation relies heavily on concentration, so before using a mandala that you have colored in, find a quiet place to sit, far from distractions or noise. Try to absorb the peaceful atmosphere around you and focus initially on stilling your mind, breathing slowly and deeply. Use the following step-by-step guide as a prompt to good practice.

HOW TO MEDITATE ON MANDALAS

1. With the chosen mandala placed on a table or on the floor at arm's length in front of you, perhaps on an improvised easel, level with your eye-line, sit comfortably—either on a chair with your feet flat on the floor, or on a cushion with your legs crossed.

2. Breathe slowly and deeply, from the diaphragm, while emptying and stilling your mind.

3. Gently gaze at the mandala and relax your eyes so that, initially, the image goes slightly out of focus.

4. Sitting quietly, concentrate fully on the image and allow its shapes, patterns and colors to work on your unconscious mind. If distracting thoughts arise, let them drift away and gently bring your focus back to the mandala.

5. Do this for at least 5 minutes initially. In later sessions, gradually try to build up your meditation period to 15 minutes.

6. When you are ready, slowly bring your attention back to the world around you.

The Sri Yantra is known as the mother of all yantras, since all other yantras derive from it. It consists of interlocking triangles, surrounded by two circles of lotus petals, all encompassed within a gated citadel. The downward-pointing triangles represent Shakti, the female principle; while the upright triangles represent Shiva, the male principle.

DREAM FLAG

THE DOUBLE WAVE SYMBOL OF THIS "VICTORIOUS FLAG OF
THE BUDDHA'S WISDOM" FIRST APPEARED TO A TIBETAN
BUDDHIST MASTER IN A VISION. IT SYMBOLIZES THE VITAL
UNION OF WISDOM AND COMPASSION.

1 First contemplate the billowing clouds. Imagine that they clouds are casting a veil over the truth that all seekers are trying to find. Like our thoughts, these obstacles to understanding are unimportant, so long as we do not *attach* too much importance to them.

2 Now shift your focus to the dream flag framed by the clouds. One half of the area, broadly speaking, denotes Heaven and spiritual insight, while the other half denotes Earth and human experience. Think of the flag as fluttering in the breeze—a marker that tells you where to find wisdom.

3 Then think in a different way about the most basic color symbolism of the flag (after you have colored it in following the recommendations given below): blue signifies wisdom; yellow, limitless compassion. The double wave brings these two qualities together—for it is the union of wisdom and compassion that enables an individual to realize their full human potential on this Earth.

RECOMMENDED COLOR PALETTE

DOUBLE WAVE SYMBOL on dream flag: On one side, **Yellow** for compassion, rootedness, earth; on the other side, **Blue** for wisdom, infinity, ascension

FRAME of dream flag: **Yellow** for compassion, rootedness, earth; with **Blue** dots for wisdom, infinity, ascension

CLOUDS: **White** for knowledge, purity, longevity; with yellow trim; against a background of blue sky

OUTER CIRCLE: **Yellow** for compassion, rootedness, earth; with **Blue** teardrops for wisdom, infinity, ascension

WHEEL OF TRUTH

THE WHEEL IS A KEY SYMBOL IN BUDDHISM, REPRESENTING BOTH THE
BUDDHA'S TEACHINGS AND ALSO THE ENDLESS CYCLE OF REBIRTH.
ONLY THROUGH THE DHARMA, AND THE REALIZATION OF TRUTH,
CAN THE CYCLE BE ESCAPED.

1 Look at the yin yang (t'ai chi) symbol at the center of this mandala. This symbol represents the complementary opposites of feminine and masculine, darkness and light, compassion and action. Each contains the seed of its opposite.

2 Extending out of the yin yang symbol are the wheel's eight spokes, symbolizing the Buddha's Eightfold Path: right view, intention, speech, action, livelihood, effort, awareness, concentration. Follow their paths out through two concentric circles before piercing the outer rim of the mandala. These circles are layers of spiritual awareness through which you advance in search of your inner truth—the ultimate liberation.

3 Take in the whole mandala and feel the strength and wisdom emanating from the wheel. Now imagine the wheel turning in a slow circle, its motion reflecting the spiritual change within you. As it turns, absorb the wheel's power into yourself.

RECOMMENDED COLOR PALETTE

YIN YANG SYMBOL: **Red** for the feminine, compassion, intuition, emotion;
White for the masculine, action, knowledge, intellect
WHEEL SPOKES: **Orange** for wisdom, strength, spirit
INNER CIRCLES: **White** for knowledge, purity, longevity
PATTERNS IN OUTER CONCENTRIC CIRCLES: Color according to your intuition, using the palette:
Red for the feminine, compassion, intuition, emotion; **Green** for balance, harmony, growth, fertility;
Blue for infinity, ascension, healing

ELEMENTAL FOUNTAIN

THIS MANDALA, WITHIN A FRAMEWORK BASED ON THE TRADITIONAL TIBETAN REPRESENTATION OF THE PALACE OF THE GODS, FEATURES THE FIVE ELEMENTS—THE FIFTH BEING SPIRIT. IN THE END WE ARE GUIDED BACK TO THE SOURCE—THE WATERS OF LIFE.

1 Gaze at the whole mandala, taking in the right-angled frame (the cosmos) as well as the innermost circle (eternity and spiritual perfection). Then think of yourself as a privileged visitor to the sacred palace. Enter the outer courtyard and feel the spiritual atmosphere seep into you.

2 Now move in deeper to the four inner pavilions, which represent the four elements—water, air, earth and fire (from noon, clockwise). These dwell in the cosmos, but also within you. Tap into their energies before progressing to the inner sanctum, whose circle is the fifth element, spirit.

3 You are now in the heart of the garden, refreshed by the waters of the fountain—the life force, endlessly flowing. Imagine the water filling you up with its spiritual goodness—feel yourself brimming with love and compassion, and let it flow out to share with the world.

RECOMMENDED COLOR PALETTE

FOUNTAIN: **Yellow** for compassion, rootedness, earth

WATER AND SQUARE PATTERN: **White** for knowledge, purity, longevity

RING AROUND FOUNTAIN: **Blue** for infinity, ascension, healing;
with **White** water drops for knowledge, purity, longevity

FOUR INNER PAVILIONS: **Green** for harmony, growth, fertility

FOUR COMPASSES: **Yellow** (standing in for gold) for holiness, the sun, enlightenment

OUTERMOST FRAME: **Red** for love, empathy, intuition

GARUDA

GARUDAS ARE HUGE BIRD-LIKE CREATURES WITH HUMAN
ARMS THAT SYMBOLIZE WISDOM IN TIBETAN BUDDHISM.
THE SNAKE DENOTES ANGER AND HATRED, AND REPRESENTS
ONE OF THE HINDRANCES THAT RESULTS IN REBIRTH.

1 Focus softly on the ring of lotus petals. Positioned on the mandala's outer edge, they suggest the possibility of nirvana, the ideal state of being. Accept this possibility as real.

2 Now take your attention to the angular, geometric shape that connects with the ring of petals. This is your earthly existence, the world of change and feeling. Be aware of any negative emotions that may swirl around here. Allow them to lift themselves off the page and disappear, out of your field of view.

3 Finally, focus on the Garuda, triumphant with the snake between its beak. Imagine your own inner wisdom swooping down in a burst of tremendous energy whenever those emotions start churning again. You are in a state of peace, your inner calm restored. You need the ferocity of the Garuda to keep yourself pure and equip you for enlightenment: he is always there to help you when you need him.

RECOMMENDED COLOR PALETTE

OUTER RING OF LOTUS PETALS: **Orange** for wisdom, spirit, enlightenment; with green leaves in between

SNAKE: **Green** for emotion, nature, ferocious energy

GARUDA'S HEAD: **Blue** for infinity, ascension, healing

GARUDA'S ARMS: **Red** for life force, protection, strength

GARUDA'S WINGS: **Yellow** for freedom, victory, solar power

GARUDA'S BODY and TAIL: Color in contrasting yellow, blue and green

BACKGROUND: Blue sky, with white clouds/smoke

PALACE OF ETERNITY

THIS IMAGE, BASED ON THE TRADITIONAL TIBETAN BUDDHIST MANDALA, REPRESENTS THE PALACE OF THE SPIRIT. ESSENTIALLY, THIS IS THE UNIVERSE IN ITS TOTALITY, WITH GATEWAYS AT EACH OF THE FOUR POINTS OF THE COMPASS FOR ALL WHO WISH TO ENTER.

1 Meditate on the wheels and flower circles within the mandala, which represent spiritual power and truth. Behind them is the symmetrical geometry of creation—the intrinsic order of existence, accessible through meditation.

2 Observing the four gateways, bear in mind that you can enter the truths of Buddhism from any direction.

3 Look at the mandala's central point, a portal to self-knowledge. Relish this first step you are taking on your inner journey. Once you can see that the journey and the destination are one, the missing element will appear like an invisible halo: the perfect circle that encloses the square like the Buddha's endless, all-encompassing compassion.

RECOMMENDED COLOR PALETTE

LOTUS FLOWERS: **Pink** for beauty, perfection, the Buddha
MANY-PETALLED FLOWERS: **Orange** for wisdom, strength, spirit
SQUARE FRAMES: **Yellow** for compassion, rootedness, earth
BACKGROUND: **Blue** for infinity, ascension, healing;
Green for balance, harmony, growth, fertility;
Red for love, empathy, intuition;
Yellow (standing in for gold) for holiness, the sun, enlightenment

PURIFYING FIRE

THIS MANDALA LOOSELY SUGGESTS THE WHEEL OF BUDDHISM—
REPRESENTING THE DHARMA. HOWEVER, THE FIRE CARRIES A FURTHER
CONNOTATION: IT'S THE PURIFYING ELEMENT THAT SYMBOLICALLY
DESTROYS SELFISH ATTACHMENTS.

1 Take in the vibrant energy of this fiery mandala. Then narrow your gaze to the incense burner at the heart of the image, which miraculously floats on a bowl of water. While the water suggests your earthly self, the flames denote your capacity for spiritual transformation. You can find this power for change within yourself if only you know how to look.

2 Let your eyes wander over the fingers of bright flames spreading out from the center—like lasers they are burning away any destructive emotions that may have taken possession of your being. Feel your worldly desires shrivel in the flames.

3 Finally, gaze upon the dark tongue-like flames encircling the mandala. Here the heat is most intense. To complete your transformation, let these flames consume the ego, leaving your spirit pure. At this point the flames generate the light of self-awareness, as your purity shines radiantly.

RECOMMENDED COLOR PALETTE

BOWL: **Brown** for groundedness, creation, tradition
WATER: **Blue** for infinity, ascension, healing
INCENSE BURNER: **Yellow** for compassion, rootedness, earth
FLAMES: **Red** for life force, love, empathy, intuition; **Orange** for wisdom, strength, spirit;
Yellow for compassion, rootedness, earth

DIAMOND THUNDERBOLT

THE DIAMOND THUNDERBOLT, OR VAJRA, SYMBOLIZES THE POWER
OF ENLIGHTENMENT—SHATTERING IGNORANCE AND DELUSION
IN A LIGHTNING BOLT OF INSIGHT. ABSORB THE ENERGIES OF THIS
MANDALA TO FORTIFY YOU DURING TIMES OF CHALLENGE OR CHANGE.

1   Fix your eyes on the central point of the mandala. This is the bindu, the point from which the mandala derives all its energy. See it as a symbol of your inner self: if you can tap into your own spiritual energy, which all of us have, you have the potential for greatness.

2   See how the thunderbolts—depicted rather like double-ended scepters (with some crossed in pairs)—streak out from the central orb, as though released by the bindu's energy. Together they represent Buddhahood and the moment of enlightenment—look at these thunderbolts bursting out through the outer cloud layer, replacing ignorance with awareness.

3   Take the whole image into your mind as an emblem of strength and truth designed to bolster and encourage your spiritual growth. Let it settle in your consciousness as a promise of a radiant future.

RECOMMENDED COLOR PALETTE

BINDU: **Yellow** for compassion, rootedness, earth; **Red** for love, empathy, intuition; **Green** for harmony, growth, fertility; **Orange** for wisdom, strength, spirit; **Blue** for infinity, ascension, healing
THUNDERBOLTS and FOUR-POINTED SCEPTERS: **Yellow** (standing in for gold) for holiness, the sun, enlightenment
CLOUD LAYER: **White** for knowledge, purity, longevity

JEWELED LOTUS

THE LOTUS REPRESENTS TRANSCENDENCE, THE ABILITY OF THE SELF
TO BLOSSOM FROM DARKNESS (THE RIVERBED) INTO LIGHT
(THE WATER'S SURFACE). ITS GROWTH SYMBOLIZES THE PATH
TRODDEN BY THE BUDDHA IN HIS JOURNEY TO ENLIGHTENMENT.

1 Fix your gaze on the jewel at the heart of the lotus flower. This represents your human potential and the value of your hidden depths. As you take in the sharp angles of the gem, feel that latent power stir inside you, poised to grow and flourish like a flower.

2 Now move your eyes over the layers of diamond-pointed shapes that surround the lotus. Imagine these as the steps on your soul's journey that begins in the dark mud of human imperfections and, once nourished, moves gradually outward toward the light as your inner beauty blossoms.

3 Finally, let your focus move inward again to take in the glorious design of the lotus flower. Its beauty is born from the very core of the self and shimmers with the radiance of your spirit. This is the inspiration for your personal destiny, and the focus for your spiritual development.

RECOMMENDED COLOR PALETTE

JEWEL: **White** (standing in for silver) for chastity, eloquence, potential

STAMENS: **Yellow** for compassion, rootedness, earth

LOTUS PETALS: **Pink** for beauty, perfection, the Buddha

LAYERS OF PENTAGONAL SHAPES: **Green** (dark and light shades if available) for harmony, growth, fertility

WATCHFUL PEACOCK

ALTHOUGH IN THE WEST THE PEACOCK IS ASSOCIATED WITH
VANITY, IN THE EAST IT SYMBOLIZES IMMORTALITY, PURITY AND—
THANKS TO THE EYE-LIKE MOTIFS IN ITS TAIL—COMPASSION,
MADE MORE EFFECTIVE BY WATCHFULNESS.

1 Gaze at the mandala, taking in its whole design. Feast your eyes on the intricate splendour of the peacock. Ponder for a while on ways to exhibit such beauty in your own life through your thoughts and actions.

2 Now focus on the peacock's eye—the very center of the mandala. Imagine yourself entering the essence of the peacock through the pupil of this eye, and losing yourself. Beyond the surface of the mandala you reconnect with your true awareness. Your ego has been left behind.

3 Shift your gaze out through the bands of plumage, to the "eyes" of the glorious, outspread tail. Contemplate the delicate lines of the feathers and relish their lovely tracery. Such close attention to detail generates compassion: by being watchful you will notice and act upon all occasions to give selfless love to your fellow human beings.

RECOMMENDED COLOR PALETTE

PEACOCK'S EYE: **Green** for harmony, growth, fertility
TAIL BASE: **Yellow** for compassion, rootedness, earth; with green edging
OUTER TAIL: **Green** for harmony, growth, fertility; with blue, purple and orange "eyes"
PEACOCK'S HEAD and FEET: **Pink** for beauty, perfection, the Buddha
PEACOCK'S COLLAR: **Blue** for infinity, ascension, healing
PEACOCK'S BREAST: **Purple** for spirituality, mysticism, creativity

COSMIC EYE

THIS MANDALA SHOWS BOTH THE COSMOS AND THE PUPIL OF A HUMAN EYE—A VISUAL AMBIGUITY THAT PUTS US IN MIND OF WHAT WU-MEN SAID IN 13TH-CENTURY CHINA: "WHEN YOU SEE THROUGH AN INSTANT OF ETERNITY, YOU SEE THROUGH THE ONE WHO SEES."

1 Contemplate the outer circles of the mandala—representing the elements and all creation. These exist within the circle of eternity: understand this, and you take the first step inward toward the ultimate truth.

2 Now look at the interconnecting inner circles, reflecting the energies of the cosmos in dynamic balance with each other. This is samsara, the world of endless change. To escape unhappiness we must travel further into the heart of silence.

3 Lastly, enter the pupil of the eye—which is also the still center of the turning wheel of life. Here, forget the paradox of seeing the eye that sees, and find the stillness at the heart of all being.

RECOMMENDED COLOR PALETTE

EYE'S PUPIL: **Black** for infinity, mystery, potential

INTERCONNECTING CIRCLES: **Red** for love, empathy, intuition; **Blue** for infinity, ascension, healing; **White** for knowledge, purity, longevity; **Yellow** for compassion, rootedness, earth; **Green** for harmony, growth, fertility

OUTER CIRCLES (from innermost to outermost): **Blue** for infinity, ascension, healing; **Red** for love, empathy, intuition; **Yellow** for compassion, rootedness, earth

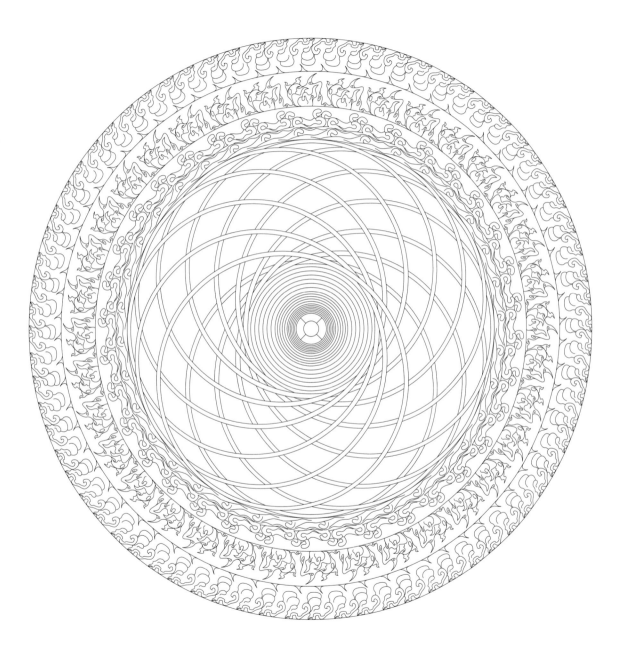

WHEEL OF DHARMA

THE "TURNINGS OF THE WHEEL OF DHARMA" ARE THE
PROGRESSIVELY MORE COMPLEX STAGES OF THE
BUDDHA'S TEACHINGS. MEDITATE ON THIS MANDALA
TO FIND DEEPER LAYERS OF AWARENESS.

1 Let your eyes travel freely over the mandala. The microcosm of your inner world is enclosed within the larger circle, while outside this is the macrocosm, denoted by the imagery of nature. Meditate for a moment on the union of these two spheres of being. Inner and outer are all part of the same oneness.

2 Focus on the wheel of dharma, which can deepen your knowledge of the self and connect you with the ultimate truths. The hub of the wheel symbolizes discipline, the eight spokes symbolize the Buddha's Eightfold Path (see page 8) and the circular rim of the wheel symbolizes spiritual perfection.

3 Now take your attention back to the hub, and revolve the wheel inside your mind with conscious mental effort. To turn the wheel by the rim is easier, but this wheel must be powered from the center. Feel your life becoming radiant as you start to turn the wheel of dharma and move farther along your path.

RECOMMENDED COLOR PALETTE

WHEEL and DEER: **Yellow** for compassion, rootedness, earth

CLOUDS: **White** for knowledge, purity, longevity

FOUR "TEARDROP" SHAPES: **Orange** for wisdom, strength, spirit

LOTUS FLOWER: **Pink** for beauty, perfection, the Buddha

CLUSTERS OF FLOWERS and BACKGROUND BEHIND WHEEL: **Blue** for infinity, ascension, healing

TREE OF ENLIGHTENMENT

WHEN THE BUDDHA ATTAINED ENLIGHTENMENT
UNDER THE BODHI TREE, HE LEFT TWO FOOTPRINTS WHICH
COMMEMORATE THAT MOMENT. BOTH TREE AND FOOTPRINTS
ARE IMPORTANT IMAGES IN BUDDHIST SYMBOLISM.

1 Start your meditation by looking at the double tree with its shared roots. These roots represent the self, nourished by the earth, while the two trunks, sharing one leaf canopy, represent the mind and body. Consider the leaves as your potential for spiritual awakening.

2 Think further about the implications of the shared roots and leaves. If we follow in the footsteps of the Buddha, each of us can attain enlightenment and enter nirvana, however individual our journey. Then turn your gaze to the birds, which suggest the heart's freedom and the spirit's ability to fly.

3 Finally, move your eyes to the outer edge of the mandala, and follow the footprints of the Buddha around in a circle. The path they tread may be long, but enlightenment can come without warning— take strength and inspiration from these signs left by the great teacher.

RECOMMENDED COLOR PALETTE

BIRDS: One **Red** for love, empathy, intuition; the other **Orange** for wisdom, strength, spirit

TREE TRUNK and BRANCHES: **Brown** for groundedness, creation, tradition

LEAVES: **Green** for harmony, growth, fertility

EARTH and CIRCLE OF FEET: **Yellow** for compassion, rootedness, earth

HEART LOTUS

THE HEART IS THE MIDDLE POINT IN OUR SYSTEM OF CHAKRAS
(ENERGY CENTERS) WITHIN THE BODY. IT IS THE SOURCE FROM WHICH
LOVE AND COMPASSION EMANATE. THE LOTUS SUGGESTS SPIRITUALITY,
WHICH WE CAN FIND IN OUR HEARTS.

1 Look at the concentric circles that frame the mandala, which denote spiritual perfection. This is the true state of being, accessible to all if only we can open our hearts.

2 Then contemplate the leaves and petals of the lotus, which continue this symbolism. The lotus can flower within ourselves and enable us to transcend suffering. As we flower spiritually, our hearts spill out love and compassion—tender as the lotus petals, strong as the life-force itself.

3 Lastly, gaze at the central hexagram, with its intersecting triangles, representing the dualities of existence. To open the pure heart fully, we must bring into balance the complementary aspects of our life—male and female, light and shadow, mind and body, practicality and spirituality.

4 Soften your gaze and let the mandala de-focus slightly. Allow it to rest gently in your mind, floating on the stillness within, and emanating deeper stillness, with love at its core.

RECOMMENDED COLOR PALETTE

CENTRAL HEXAGRAM: **Yellow** for compassion, rootedness, earth

LOTUS PETALS and OUTER CONCENTRIC CIRCLES: **Pink** for beauty, perfection, the Buddha

HEART CHAKRA WITHIN HEXAGRAM and BACKGROUND TO LOTUS PETALS: **Red** for love, empathy, intuition

LEAVES: **Green** for harmony, growth, fertility

SRI YANTRA

THIS IS A SIMPLIFIED VERSION OF THE SACRED HINDU
SRI YANTRA. ITS PATTERN OF INTERLINKING TRIANGLES HAS
A COMPELLING MYSTIC BEAUTY, REPRESENTING THE TIMELESS
CREATIVITY OF THE UNIVERSE.

1 Focus on the center of the mandala and its opposing sets of triangles—these represent the male and female principles which, in their fusion, give rise to creation.

2 Now turn your attention to the geometry surrounding the image. Consider the equal-armed cross, whose elements represent the created cosmos, and the circle, denoting spiritual perfection. Contemplate also the lotus leaves—four in the corners of the square, and a long succession of them all around the circular frame. These are a promise of spiritual growth, the attainment of true awareness.

3 Turn your attention to the very center of the Sri Yantra, where the bindu (focal point) would normally be found. This is the source of all creation. As your own mind absorbs this yantra into itself, it experiences the unfolding of the cosmos and the union of all creation—past, present and future.

RECOMMENDED COLOR PALETTE

UPWARD-POINTING TRIANGLES: **Blue** for the feminine, infinity, ascension, healing
DOWNWARD-POINTING TRIANGLES: **Yellow** for the masculine, rootedness, earth
INNER CIRCLE: **Yellow** (standing in for gold) for holiness, the sun, enlightenment
RING OF LOTUS PETALS and OUTERMOST CORNERS OF SQUARE: **Red** for love, empathy, intuition
FOUR-DIRECTIONED SQUARE: **Blue** for infinity, ascension, healing
BACKGROUND: **Purple** for spirituality, mysticism, creativity

LOVING KINDNESS

THIS TIBETAN-INSPIRED MANDALA ENABLES YOU TO SUFFUSE YOUR WHOLE MIND WITH POSITIVE FEELINGS TOWARD OTHERS —NOT ONLY LOVED ONES AND FRIENDS, BUT ALSO ACQUAINTANCES AND EVEN STRANGERS.

1 Imagine a loved one sitting in the mandala's center, where the seated figure is. Dwell on the qualities you admire so much in this person. Visualize him or her bathed in your love.

2 Contemplate the four symbols within the 'T' shapes: dove (peace), hands (warmth), fire (purity) and eye (empathy). Identify all these ingredients in the quality of your love.

3 Visualize family and friends in particular niches inside the mandala. Beyond the central square are mere acquaintances and beyond the outer circle a number of strangers.

4 Welling up around the central figure and endlessly spilling outward, feel your love pouring out of you and energizing everyone. The strangers receive the same quality of love as your loved one—a love that is undiminished by distance.

RECOMMENDED COLOR PALETTE

CLOTHES OF CENTRAL FIGURE, INNER PETALS (containing figures) and LARGER CIRCLES: **Red** for love, empathy, intuition
FOUR-DIRECTIONED SQUARE and SPIRAL PATTERN: **Blue** for infinity, ascension, healing
OUTER FLOATING CIRCLES: **Purple** for spirituality, mysticism, creativity
DOVE (in top arm of square): **White** for knowledge, purity, longevity
HANDS (in right arm of square): **Yellow** for compassion, rootedness, earth
EYE (in left arm of square): **Green** for harmony, growth, fertility
FIRE (in lower arm of square): **Orange** for wisdom, strength, spirit

AVALOKITESHVARA

THIS IS THE NAME GIVEN IN TANTRIC BUDDHISM TO THE
BODHISATTVA (ENLIGHTENED BEING) OF COMPASSION. HE RADIATES
SELF-SACRIFICING LOVE—DENYING HIMSELF ENTRY TO NIRVANA
UNTIL ALL OTHERS CAN ENTER AS WELL.

1 Any depiction of Avalokiteshvara compels our gaze and demands our profound admiration. Feel the energy of his goodness. It is this that enables us to accept a one-dimensional painting as a deeply benevolent presence.

2 The *bodhisattva* sits cross-legged upon a lotus flower. Contemplate the perfection he has chosen as his setting.

3 Two of Avalokiteshvara's hands express devotion, while the other two hold a rosary and a lotus. The rosary enables him to count the repetitions of his mantra, *"Om Mani Padme Hum"*, which liberates all beings from suffering. He is weightless, like an image in a mirror. He transcends all concepts—including the idea that he exists only in another dimension. Meditate and you will find him inside yourself.

RECOMMENDED COLOR PALETTE

BODHISATTVA'S ROBES, EARRINGS and CROWN: **Orange** for wisdom, strength, spirit
BODHISATTVA'S HALO: **Green** for harmony, growth, fertility; with **Orange** border for wisdom, strength, spirit
BODHISATTVA'S SKIN and CLOUD LAYERS: **White** for knowledge, purity, longevity
OVAL FRAME AROUND BODHISATTVA: **Red** for love, empathy, intuition
LOTUS FLOWERS IN CORNERS and BASE OF PETALS: **Pink** for beauty, perfection, the Buddha
WATER: **Blue** for infinity, ascension, healing; use a lighter blue for the sky if available

FIRE AROUND THE LOTUS

HERE THE DEEPLY SPIRITUAL LOTUS IS SURROUNDED BY A RING OF FIRE, SUGGESTING PURIFICATION. THIS MANDALA ALSO SHOWS A FOUR-GATED PALACE, DENOTING SHELTER OR SAFETY, UNIVERSAL ORDER AND THE BALANCE OF OPPOSITES.

1 Start by contemplating the outer ring of fire—a complex symbol with overtones of purification through destruction, the light of wisdom and regeneration. You are not afraid to burn off your attachments.

2 Now look at the lotus, which flowers within your mind as your spiritual vision becomes focused. With its roots in the mud, the lotus in its growth and blossoming aspires to heavenly enlightenment. Feel this adventure of fulfilment within yourself, and take strength from it.

3 Lastly, take your mind into the four-gated palace at the heart of the mandala. Awakened as you are, you will find the emptiness of the palace immeasurably rich and nourishing. You have no need of the material, the tangible. You are deeply at peace with yourself and with the cosmos.

RECOMMENDED COLOR PALETTE

FOUR CENTRAL GATES: **Purple** for spirituality, mysticism, creativity; against a **White** background for knowledge, purity, longevity

CENTRAL CIRCLE and LEAVES: **Green** for harmony, growth, fertility

LOTUS PETALS: **Blue** for infinity, ascension, healing

OUTER RINGS OF FIRE: **Red** for love, empathy, intuition; **Orange** for wisdom, strength, spirit

PALACE OF THE GODS

TRADITIONAL MANDALAS WERE OFTEN SEEN AS DIAGRAMS OF
THE PALACE OF THE GODS. THIS MODERN VERSION SHOWS A PLAN
OF THE PALACE AND SIDE-ON VIEWS OF EIGHT PAVILIONS.
THE PALACE IS BOTH THE COSMOS AND THE SELF.

1 In your mind enter the sacred palace gardens, as defined by the outer circle of the mandala. Here you are outside time and space. The large circle and the smaller ones inside it generate a spiritual atmosphere.

2 Think of the four pavilions in the outer wall of the palace as the domain of earth, air, fire and water. All four elements dwell in the mandala, in the cosmos and in your own self. The fifth element, ether or spirit, has its own inner enclosure, at the very center of the mandala. Enter the inner square now. Once inside, you are able to transcend earthly barriers (the concentric square walls) and bathe in the sacred fountain.

3 The fountain flows inside you endlessly, the life-force that sustains your being. It is blessed by the divine, and brings infinite peace to your spirit.

RECOMMENDED COLOR PALETTE

FOUNTAIN and FOUR WHEELS: **Yellow** (standing in for gold) for holiness, the sun, enlightenment

WATER: **Blue** for infinity, ascension, healing

FOUR INNER PAVILIONS and WALLS: **Yellow** (standing in for gold) for holiness, the sun, enlightenment

FOUR OUTER PAVILIONS: One **Brown** for earth; one **White** for air; one **Red** for fire; one **Blue** for water

FLOWER-PATTERNED BACKGROUND: Color according to your discretion. Use the palette:

Red for life force, love, empathy, intuition; **Orange** for wisdom, strength, spirit;

Green for balance, harmony, growth, fertility; **White** for knowledge, purity, longevity

TIME AND THE UNIVERSE

THINKING ABOUT THE NATURE OF TIME CAN PRODUCE CONFUSION, EVEN DESPAIR. FORGETTING THE CLOCK AND SEEING TIME AS THE ETERNAL FLOW OF THE UNIVERSE IS A REASSURING AND REFRESHING VISUAL MEDITATION.

1 Identify the elements of the mandala: time as a flow, the river changeless yet endlessly changing; the seasons; the movements of the stars, Earth, sun and moon; the four symbols of the butterfly (which has a briefer life than ours), the tree (which has a longer life than ours), the spiral (infinite time) and the Möbius strip (infinite space).

2 Still holding the mandala in your field of view, imagine all the separate meanings of these different aspects of time dissolving into the great river, the flow of the cosmos.

3 Feel yourself entering the great river of time, interfusing with its flow: the river is within you and you are within the river. The mandala is a drop of water, one of an infinite number of such drops. Relax into the endlessness of time and space.

RECOMMENDED COLOR PALETTE

WATER: **Blue** for infinity, ascension, healing; with **White** foam for knowledge, purity, longevity

PETALS (containing symbols): **Red** for love, empathy, intuition

UPPER LEAF: **Green** for harmony, growth, fertility

LOWER LEAF: **Brown** for groundedness, creation, tradition

STARS: **Yellow** for holiness, mystery, enlightenment

SUN: **Orange** for wisdom, strength, spirit

TRANSFORMATIONS

THIS MANDALA USES IMAGERY DERIVED ENTIRELY FROM NATURE. BUTTERFLIES DENOTE TRANSFORMATION—OUR AWAKENING FROM THE DOMINANCE OF THE EGO TO A MATURE SELF-AWARENESS. LOVE ENABLES US TO TURN OUR ENERGIES BOTH INWARD (TO TRUTH) AND OUTWARD (TO COMPASSION).

1 Look at the butterflies in the image and choose one at random. Mentally trace its life-cycle back through the different phases: butterfly back to chrysalis, chrysalis back to caterpillar, caterpillar back to egg. Think of time as a circle within the boundlessness of eternity: you can travel either forwards or backwards at will, into the past or into the future.

2 Next focus on the caterpillar in the center of the mandala. Think of the potential for radical change inherent in the creature. Its destiny lies within itself, like a coil of time waiting to be unwound.

3 Turn your attention to the four butterflies emerging from their chrysalises—change is now taking place, the promise is starting to be fulfilled.

4 Now think of this potential for transformation in the very part of yourself that absorbs the image of the mandala. Sense your capacity for giving and receiving love in abundance, and relish the blessings that such compassion will bring you.

5 Soften your gaze, and take the mandala as a whole into your mind—a promise of your infinite capacity for fulfilment.

RECOMMENDED COLOR PALETTE

CATERPILLAR: **Brown** for groundedness, creation, tradition
INNER CIRCLE OF LEAVES: **Blue** for infinity, ascension, healing
BUTTERFLIES: Multi-colored; color according to your own intuition.
Include **Red** for love, empathy, intuition; **Yellow** for compassion, rootedness, earth
OUTER CIRCLE OF LEAVES: **Green** for balance, harmony, growth, fertility

CRANES AMONG CLOUDS

IN THE JAPANESE TRADITION CRANES ARE SYMBOLS OF GOOD FORTUNE.
CLOUDS REMIND US OF THE CHANCE EVENTS THAT TEMPORARILY
CAST SHADOWS OVER OUR LIVES. THIS MEDITATION COMBINES
THESE EVOCATIVE SYMBOLS.

1   Identify the main elements of the mandala—the cranes, the blue sky, the clouds that sometimes block flying cranes from our view. In the corners of the mandala is the ocean, over which the cranes fly on migration.

2   Turn your gaze to the clouds that form a circular pattern against the sky. Imagine them floating across your consciousness. Visualize the loose flock of cranes flying in and out of the clouds randomly. Each crane that appears brings blessings into your life. Some of the cranes fly right through the clouds—like a happy outcome emerging from a risky situation. Give thanks for such good fortune.

3   Soften your gaze, and let the whole mandala rest gently in your mind, its energies bringing you peace and fulfilment.

RECOMMENDED COLOR PALETTE

CRANES: **White** for knowledge, purity, longevity; with yellow for the outer wings;
black for the tail and throat; red for the crest
CLOUD LAYERS: **White** for knowledge, purity, longevity
INNER and OUTER CIRCLES: Color the segments alternately:
Green for harmony, growth, fertility; **Orange** for wisdom, strength, spirit
SKY: **Blue** for infinity, ascension, healing
OCEAN: **Blue** with green edging

JEWELS

GEMS WERE OBJECTS OF WONDER TO THE ANCIENTS, DIVINE FORCES CONJURING LIGHT FROM DARK EARTH. IN EASTERN THOUGHT, JEWELS SIGNIFIED SPIRITUAL ILLUMINATION. THIS BEJEWELED MANDALA CONTAINS ONE CENTRAL AND FOUR SUBSIDIARY YIN YANG (T'AI CHI) SYMBOLS, TOO.

1   Look at the different jewels and their colors. There are diamonds, denoting radiance and integrity; rubies, denoting love and courage; pearls, denoting intuition and feminine wisdom; sapphires, denoting peace and harmony; emeralds, denoting ascension and healing.

2   See the pattern of the jewels in their delicate settings as being symbolic of the radiant and intricate order of the universe, illuminated by the intensely beautiful light of the spirit.

3   Let your eyes rest on the yin yang symbol—the creative interplay of opposites at the heart of our existence. The spirit adorns and transcends the body, as the jewels adorn and transcend male and female, light and dark, action and feeling.

RECOMMENDED COLOR PALETTE

YIN YANG SYMBOLS: **Blue** for the masculine, infinity, ascension, healing;
White for the feminine, knowledge, purity, longevity
SPOKES and DECORATIVE FRAME: **Yellow** (standing in for gold) for holiness, the sun, enlightenment
JEWELS: **White** for pearls; **Green** for emeralds; **Red** for rubies; **Blue** for sapphires; **Pink** for diamonds

THE LOTUS AND THE PINE

HERE IS ANOTHER MANDALA BASED ON EASTERN SYMBOLISM.
THE LOTUS SUGGESTS ENLIGHTENMENT; THE OLD PINE TREE SUGGESTS
LONGEVITY OR OLD AGE. ENLIGHTENMENT CAN COME AT ANY TIME.
WHENEVER IT OCCURS, WE HAPPILY ACCEPT—NAY, EMBRACE—IN OUR
ENLIGHTENED STATE THE INEVITABILITY OF PHYSICAL DECLINE.

1 First, look at the gnarled pine trees around the circular frame of the mandala, and see them as a group of people who are our contemporaries in old age—everyone mellow and beautiful with antiquity.

2 Imagine moving from the clustered pine trees to the pond in the center of the forest. This is where the lotus of enlightenment blooms with its roots in the mud—perhaps the mud is the reality of transience, the fact that all living things have their time.

3 Look at the beautiful lotus flower and see enlightenment blossoming in your mind, in the same way that the lotus petals have opened in their watery home. Feel the unfolding of petals inside your consciousness as you sit with your gaze still focused on the lotus.

RECOMMENDED COLOR PALETTE

LOTUS FLOWER: **Pink** for beauty, perfection, the Buddha; with a **Yellow** center for compassion, rootedness, earth

PINE TREES: **Black** for knowledge, antiquity, truth

INNER PATTERNED RINGS: **Purple** for spirituality, mysticism, creativity; with **Pink** highlights

BIRDS: **Orange** for wisdom, strength, spirit

BACKGROUND: **Blue** for infinity, ascension, healing

A DIAMOND'S LIGHT

GEMSTONES BETOKEN THE GIFTS OF LIFE AND CONSCIOUSNESS—
LIGHT EMERGING MIRACULOUSLY FROM THE DARK OF EARTH.
INDIAN ALCHEMISTS REGARDED THE DIAMOND AS THE ULTIMATE GOAL
OF THEIR PRACTICES: IMMORTALITY. TANTRIC BUDDHISTS SAW THE
DIAMOND'S HARDNESS AS ANALOGOUS TO SPIRITUAL FORCE.

1   Start by contemplating the geometric framework of this mandala—the circle symbolizing eternity and the interlocking squares denoting the created world. All eight points of the two squares touch the circle—when eternity is glimpsed from within the prison of time, the prison walls dissolve.

2   Now, turn your gaze to the decorative framework within which the central diamond sits. Spiritual understanding requires a gracious setting of good, loving thoughts and selfless actions.

3   Take the scintillating radiance of the diamond deep into your mind, and let it lie there as a reflection of your blossoming self, the flowering of being beyond becoming. Feel its spiritual force—the cutting edge of enlightenment.

RECOMMENDED COLOR PALETTE

LARGE CIRCLE and OVERLAPPING SQUARES: **Yellow** for compassion, rootedness, earth
CENTRAL DIAMOND and GEMSTONES IN LARGE CIRCLE: **Pink** for beauty, perfection, the Buddha
SMALL DIAMONDS IN SQUARE FRAMES: **White** for knowledge, purity, longevity
CIRCULAR PATTERN AROUND DIAMOND: **Blue** for infinity, ascension, healing; **White** for knowledge, purity, longevity
RADIAL PATTERNS: Choose an alternation of colors according to your intuition

FLOWING WITH THE STREAM

THE TAO TE CHING PLACES GREAT EMPHASIS ON THE INEVITABLE FLOW OF NATURE—THE TAO ITSELF, IN WHICH WE MUST ALL IMMERSE OURSELVES. THIS INVOLVES SURRENDERING ALL POINTLESS RESISTANCE TO CHANGE AND ALLOWING NATURE TO TAKE ITS COURSE. HERE IS A MEDITATION ON THIS TAOIST IDEA.

1 Look at this image of streams meandering among rocks as if you were looking down upon the scene from a high mountain peak. You see the waters swirling around great boulders as they flow in different directions but inexorably bound toward the sea.

2 Think about which element—water or rock—best expresses the essential truth of human life. If we petrify to become a boulder, we will lifelessly endure. If we dissolve into water, we will flow and endlessly change until, one day, we reach the source.

3 Trace the path of the four streams outward across the rock-strewn landscape. Where the waters crash directly against a rock, there is turbulence. Where the waters yield and "step aside", there is movement—which is the quintessence of life.

RECOMMENDED COLOR PALETTE

ROCKS: **Brown** for security, reliability, rigidity

WATER: **Blue** for destiny, change, vitality; with white edging

FISHES: **Orange** for wisdom, strength, spirit

OUTER CIRCLE: **Purple** for spirituality, mysticism, creativity

Add other colors according to your intuition

LADY OF COMPASSION

COMPASSION IS THE ROOT OF SPIRITUAL HEALING. IT IS PERSONALIZED HERE AS THE GODDESS OF COMPASSION, WHO DELAYED HER OWN SALVATION UNTIL SHE HAD SAVED ALL SOULS ON EARTH. SHE IS DEPICTED IN A MEDITATION POSE, SENDING HER LOVING-KINDNESS OUTWARD FROM A HEART FULL OF LOVE.

1 Focus on the Goddess of Compassion in the center of the mandala. Open your heart to her unconditional love and acceptance. Feel confident that her endless compassion is pouring out to you, enabling you to be compassionate in turn.

2 Now rest in the ring of soft, heart-shaped petals. Feel the blooming of compassion inside yourself, like a warm glow.

3 Let your eyes drift to the little circles and imagine that each one contains a miniature deity. The Goddess of Compassion's tiny form can nestle inside every human heart, including yours. Think of this goddess as residing within every atom of every in-breath and out-breath you take.

4 Take your gaze to the mandala's surround, the lovely flowers that bloom when compassion's seeds fall on fertile soil.

RECOMMENDED COLOR PALETTE

GODDESS OF COMPASSION'S CLOTHES: **Green** for balance, harmony, growth, fertility
FLOWERS WITHIN CENTRAL CIRCLE: **White** for knowledge, purity, longevity; against a green background
LARGE PETALS WITHIN MIDDLE RING: **Pink** for beauty, perfection, the Buddha; with white background
OUTER RING: **Blue** for infinity, ascension, healing; **Green** for balance, harmony, growth, fertility
For other areas use green, pink and blue according to your intuition

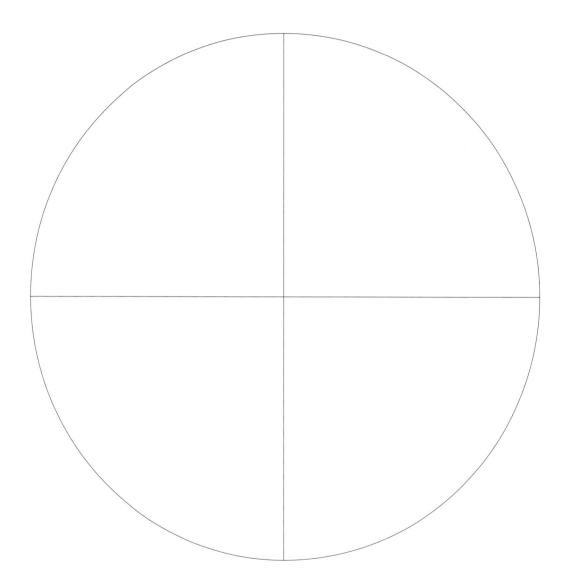

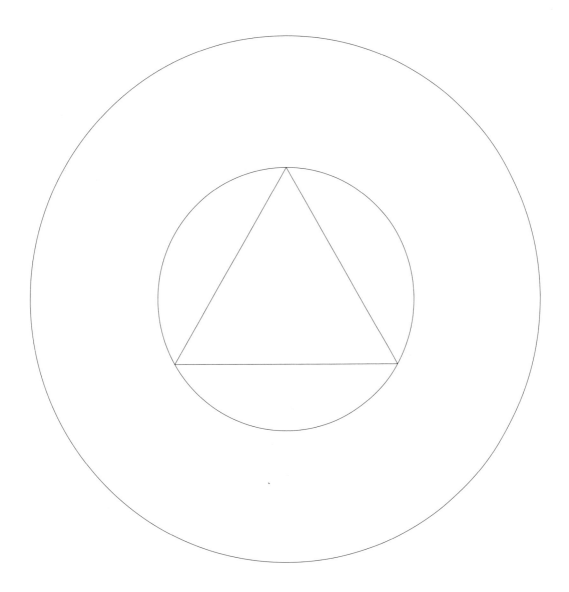

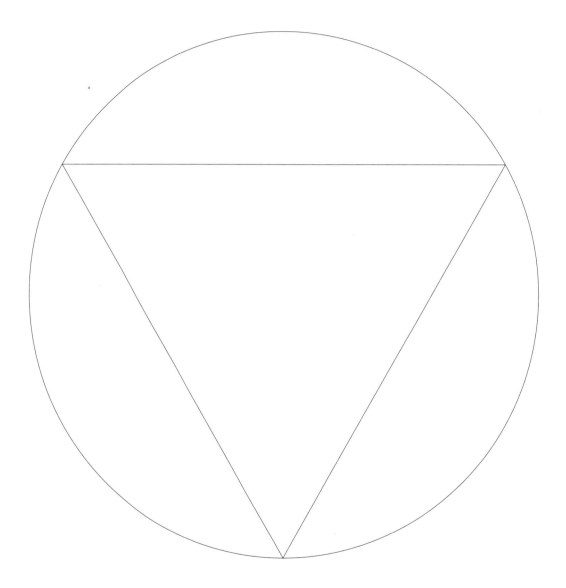

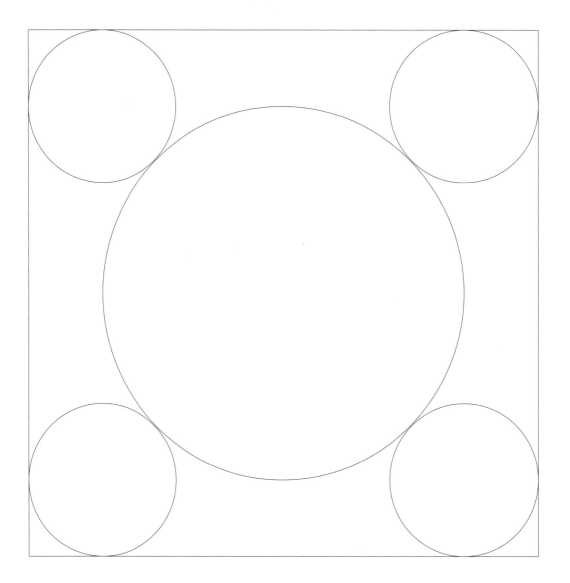

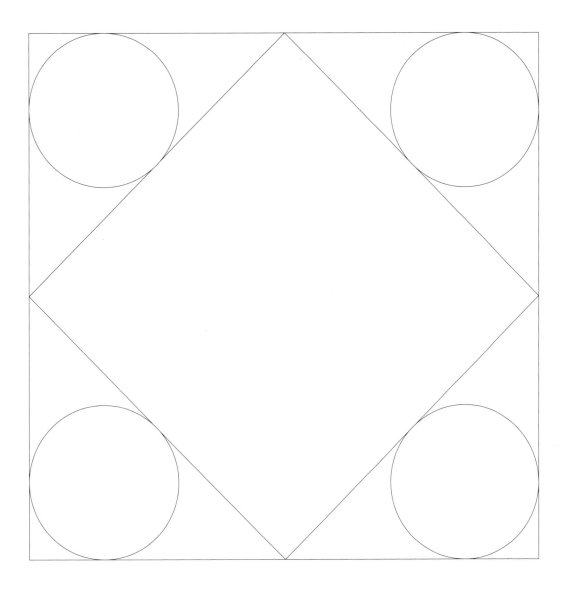

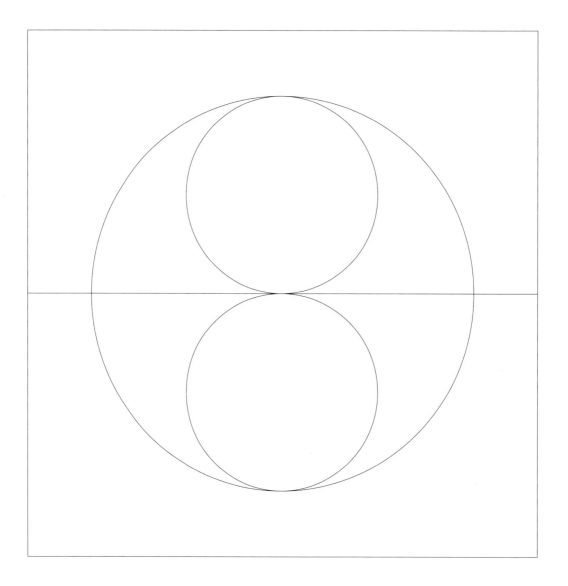

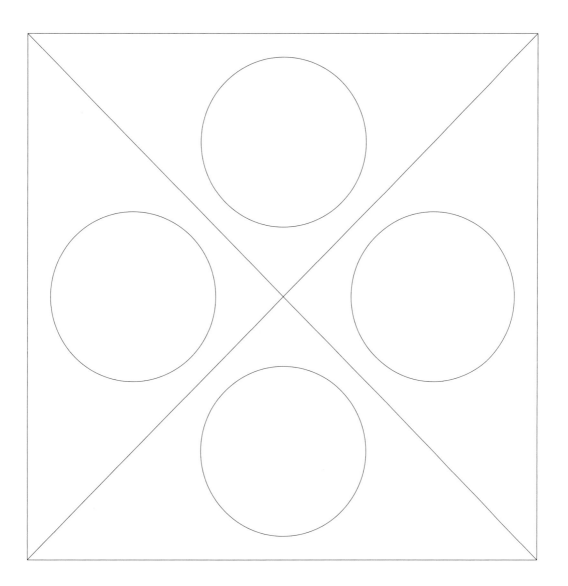

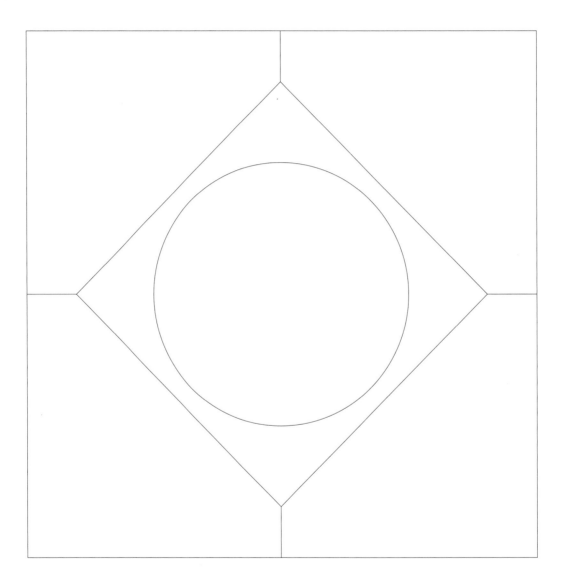

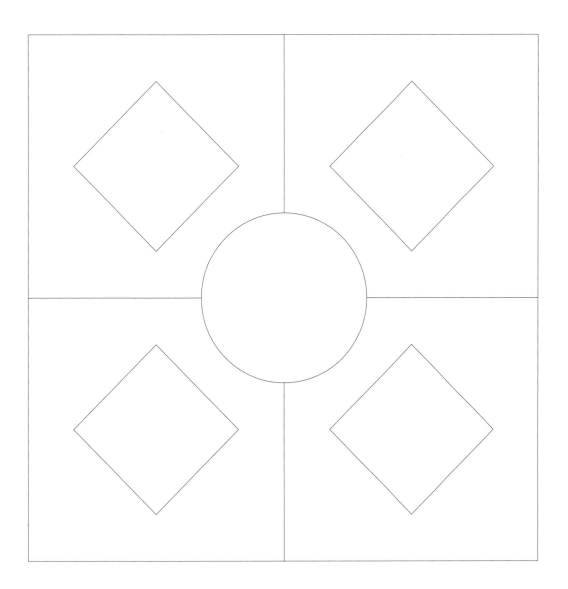

SYMBOLS OF TRUTH

It is only since the 1st century AD that the Buddha has been depicted in human form: before then he was represented by, for example, his footprints, as a mark of respect. As Buddhist traditions evolved, a rich and diverse symbolism was established to represent the Buddha's characteristics, the significant moments in his life and aspects of the dharma. The figure of the "Awakened One" is an inspiration for all followers of the Buddhist faith, yet Buddhist culture also has many specific symbols that illustrate aspects of the teachings.

The circle is the shape common to most mandalas, suggesting both the endless cycle of life (the wheel) and the state of wholeness to which believers aspire. It is also symbolic of the perfection of the dharma— the Buddha's teachings. Concentric circles within a mandala can denote layers of spiritual awareness. The spiral is another important shape, its interconnected pattern symbolizing the linked forces of wisdom and compassion. Footprints signify the enduring presence of the transcendent Buddha, and depictions of his eyes denote his all-seeing nature.

Natural imagery is often portrayed. Two important examples are the lotus flower, symbolizing purity or transcendence, and the bo or bodhi (enlightenment) tree, beneath which the Buddha sat and meditated. The four elements represent aspects of our inner nature: earth symbolizes health and material being; air stands for the mind and the power of thought; water for the ebb and flow of emotions; and fire for inspiration and transformation. Buddhists also believe in a fifth element—aether—associated with the spiritual realm. Animals feature strongly: deer commemorate the Buddha's first sermon in Sarnath Deer Park and the elephant symbolizes his power, while the lion indicates his majesty and, when roaring, the spreading of the dharma. The pig, the snake and the rooster all represent the vices that condemn an individual to samsara (rebirth)—the pig symbolizing delusion, the rooster lust, and the snake hatred and anger (all are typically found in depictions of the Wheel of Life).

Objects are also used to convey meaning. An empty throne denotes the Buddha's importance and his renunciation of royalty; stupas (Buddhist shrines) symbolize his death and entry into nirvana (escape from the imprisoning cycle of birth and rebirth); the wheel signifies the dharma; and the Three Jewels suggest the three fundamental aspects of the Buddhist faith in which believers take refuge: the Buddha, the dharma and the monastic community.

Traditional mandalas, often created by Buddhist monks, can be highly elaborate representations of nirvana and take weeks to create. Some of the most

impressive of these are made from colored sand. Once the mandala has fulfilled its purpose, the sand is then dispersed. While the physical mandala is ephemeral, the meditative effects on the practitioner are long-lasting. Although some Buddhist mandalas are extremely complex in their imagery and symbolism, the basic premise of this book is that a modern mandala, displaying more accessible symbolism, will be more suitable for today's Western practitioner, or indeed for anyone seeking spiritual wisdom or guidance.

DIRECTORY OF BUDDHIST MANDALA SYMBOLS

Many symbols within Buddhism take their significance from the specific tradition in which they are found. For example, the earliest symbols, which appeared in ancient India, occur in Hinduism as well—but often with a slightly different significance. Although the Buddha lived around the 6th century BC, no Buddhist artefacts are known before the 3rd century BC. In the scriptures there are references to the master's occasional use of images like the "Wheel of Life" to make his teachings more accessible or vivid. The earliest type of Buddhist monument is the *stupa*, a dome-shaped structure used to house sacred relics. With the growth of Buddhist Tantra around the 6th century, new kinds of symbolism evolved, reflecting the use of imagery as a tool for meditation. There was a complex pantheon of deities and protectors, which modern Buddhists often find bewildering and irrelevant. At the same time, significance was attached to symbolic objects such as the *vajra* (thunderbolt), an emblem of spiritual power; and the bell, which symbolizes wisdom.

Meditation pose
The pose of this goddess embodies the loving-kindness of all Buddhas.

Diamond thunderbolt
This is the vajra, combining the indestructability of a diamond with the force of thunder.

Fountain
At the center of the palace of the gods is a fountain of wisdom and refreshment.

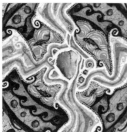

Streams
To be a rock in a stream is to resist destiny: it is more accepting to bend like a reed.

Lotus
With its roots in the mud, the lotus aspires to the heavens—an image of spiritual purity.

Samsara
The cycle of birth, suffering, death and rebirth, from which enlightenment offers escape.

Sri Yantra
A popular form of mandala in Tibetan Buddhism, which has profound cosmic meaning.

Cosmos
The wisdom of Buddhism is all-enveloping: the micro within the macro; the self within eternity.

Snowflake
Zen Buddhism finds beauty and poignancy in the passing moment. All joys are fleeting.

Dream Flag
The victory banner is a Tibetan symbol of the Buddha's triumph over ignorance and suffering.

Throne
The throne is a reference to the Buddha's royal birth, as well as to spiritual kingship.

Change
Change is a characteristic of all life: the caterpillar's existence is brief. To resist change is futile.

Wheel of Dharma
A symbol of Buddhist teachings, offered to the Buddha by the great god Brahma.

Yin Yang (T'ai Chi) symbol
A Taoist symbol used by Chinese Buddhists: the balance of opposites (yin yang).

Cranes
The crane is a bird beloved in Japan, symbolizing longevity and good fortune.

THE BUDDHIST MANDALA POCKET COLORING BOOK
LISA TENZIN-DOLMA

This edition first published in the USA and Canada in 2016 by
Watkins, an imprint of Watkins Media Limited
19 Cecil Court
London WC2N 4EZ

enquiries@watkinspublishing.co.uk

Managing Editor: Sarah Epton
Editor: Rebecca Sheppard
Managing Designer: Sailesh Patel
Commissioned Artwork: mandala color artworks by Sally
Taylor/ArtistPartners Ltd; line illustrations for mandala
templates by Studio 73; Christopher Gibbs; Rowena Dugdale

IBSN: 978-1-78028-942-7

10 9 8 7 6 5 4 3 2 1

Typeset in Novecento wide, Filosofia and Gill Sans
Printed in Slovenia

www.watkinspublishing.com

Publisher's note: This book does not recommend meditation
with mandalas for the specific treatment of any disability, only
for the enhancement of general well-being. Meditation is
beneficial for most people and generally harmless, but those
unsure of its suitability for them should consult a medical
practitioner before attempting any of the meditations in
this book. Neither the publishers nor the author can accept
responsibility for any injuries or damage incurred as a result
of following the meditations in this book, or using any of the
meditation techniques that are mentioned herein.